Yankee Doodle Riddles

American History Fun

Joan Holub

Illustrated by **Elizabeth Buttler**

Yankee Doodle
went to class,
riding in a school bus.
Wrote the riddles
in this book—
that's how he got
an A plus!

Albert Whitman
& Company
Morton Grove, Illinois

Thanks to everyone at Albert Whitman who helped, especially Heather Boyd and Carol Gildar. —J.H.

In loving memory of my mother, Ann S. Buttler, who taught me to love learning; and with much love to my father, John H. Buttler, who taught me to be true to myself. —E.A.B.

Library of Congress Cataloging-in-Publication Data

Holub, Joan.
Yankee Doodle riddles : American history fun / written by Joan Holub ;
illustrated by Elizabeth Buttler.
p. cm.
ISBN 0-8075-9260-9
1. Riddles, Juvenile. 2. United States—History—Juvenile humor. I. Buttler, Elizabeth. II. Title.
PN6371.5.H65 2003 818'.5401—dc21 2002012381

Text copyright © 2003 by Joan Holub.
Illustrations copyright © 2003 by Elizabeth Ann Buttler.
Published in 2003 by Albert Whitman & Company,
6340 Oakton Street, Morton Grove, Illinois 60053-2723.
Published simultaneously in Canada by Fitzhenry & Whiteside, Markham, Ontario.
Printed in the United States of America.
10 9 8 7 6 5 4 3 2 1

The design is by Carol Gildar.

For more information about Albert Whitman & Company,
please visit our web site at www.albertwhitman.com.

Teacher, teacher, I confess—

my history homework is a mess.

I'm truly not a history whiz.

I'll never ever pass your quiz.

So I think we should make a trade.

You take my test. I'll give the grade.

Now turn the page and do your best

to pass my history riddle test.

What's a history teacher's favorite snack?
Dates

What kind of book has snakes inside?
A hisss-tory book

When do history teachers sleep? *At maptime*

What did the history teacher name the class pet?
Abra-hamster Lincoln

A NEW LAND

Explorer

In 1492,
I sailed the ocean blue.
I flew my flags unfurled
till I reached the New World.

Who am I?

Christopher Columbus

My ships came from Spain.

My trip was a pain.

America

I sailed to the New World by sea.
I wasn't the first to do it.
They named the land there after me.
And still, my name's stuck to it.

Who am I?

Amerigo Vespucci

History Rocks!

First we docked near Plymouth Rock.
Then we boogied down and built Plymouth Town.
Our boots and shoes tapped out the news.
Now we can pray—our way. Hooray!

Who are we?

Pilgrims

What did the Pilgrims say
when Squanto showed
them how to grow corn?
How a-maize-ing!

Why were the
Pilgrims strong?
*Because they had
Mayflower power!*

March winds and April showers
bring forth May flowers.
What do Mayflowers bring?
Pilgrims

The Oldie Moldy History Library

Cracking Up
by Libby T. Bell

Amelia Earhart
by Miss Eng Still

The Boston Tea Party
by Frieda Collie Knees

The Adventures of Lewis and Clark
by X. Plorwest

The Pilgrims' Voyage to America
by May Flower

Thomas Edison's Shocking Experiment
by E. Lektrisitee

The Story of Benedict Arnold
by Ima Fink

Mixed-Up Mark Twain
by Huckleberry Sawyer

The San Francisco Earthquake
by I. Quiver

The Story of Johnny Appleseed
by Plant A. Tree

The Gettysburger Address
by Abra Ham Lincoln

The Wright Brothers
by Juan Toofly

I Helped Write the Constitution
by Pen Franklin

I Did Not Invent the Cotton Gin
by E. Lie Whitney

How Was the Wild West Fenced In?
by Barb Wire

Nine Judges
by Sue Preemcourt

Amendments
by Bill O. Wrights

George Washington Runs for President
by Betty Winz

The Story of Harriet Tubman
by Setta Sfree

The Grand Canyon
by Watt A. Landmark

The Story of Phillis Wheatley
by Poe M. Writer

What Was Said at the Salem Witch Trials?
by Ura Witch II

What Do You Get if You Cross...

The president's home with a rodent?

A White House mouse

Paul Bunyan's blue ox with Abraham Lincoln?

A Blue Babe Abe

A tornado with the Constitution?

A whooshin' Constitution

The author of <u>The Adventures of Tom Sawyer</u> with drizzle?

Mark Twain rain

A spy and a pioneer's transportation?

An under-covered wagon

Davy Crockett and an astronaut's vehicle?

A Crockett rocket

President James K. Polk with a spotted tie?

James K. Polk-a-dot

Annie Oakley and a forest?

Annie Oak tree

Daniel Boone and a song?

A Boone tune

The Alamo and a cow?

The Alamoo

Noodles and Abraham Lincoln's famous speech?

The Spaghettysburg Address

Bye-bye Britain

Party Time

Kerplunk! There goes all the tea,
right into the sea.
Splash! Dunk! Thirteen colonies
struggle to be free.

What am I?

The Boston Tea Party

Hey, King George!
Here's a surprise:
We're colonists dressed
in disguise.

Why were the British mad about the Boston Tea Party? Because they weren't invited.

This Means War!

King Georgie Porgie, puddin' and pie,
taxed the colonies and made them cry:
We won't be taxed. We will not pay.
We'll fight till Independence Day!

What am I?

The Revolutionary War

What kind of tea did
the colonists dislike?
The "t" in the word "tax."

Music Teacher: Please sing
the scales.

Colonists: Do Re Mi Fa So La–Do

Music Teacher: What happened
to the "Ti"?

Colonists: We threw it overboard.

New Taxes on:
Sugar
Tea
Coffee
Glass
(more on back)

What did the colonists wear
to the Boston Tea Party?
Tea-shirts

Good Guys

The Rider

Lanterns glowing
just for me.
Two lights warn:
Attack by sea.

Horseback riding
through the night.
Redcoats coming.
Soon we'll fight.

Who am I?

Paul Revere

What's the difference between
Paul Revere and Sir Lancelot?

*Paul Revere was a night rider,
and Sir Lancelot was a knight rider.*

Why did colonists do
everything in just 60 seconds?

Because they were Minutemen.

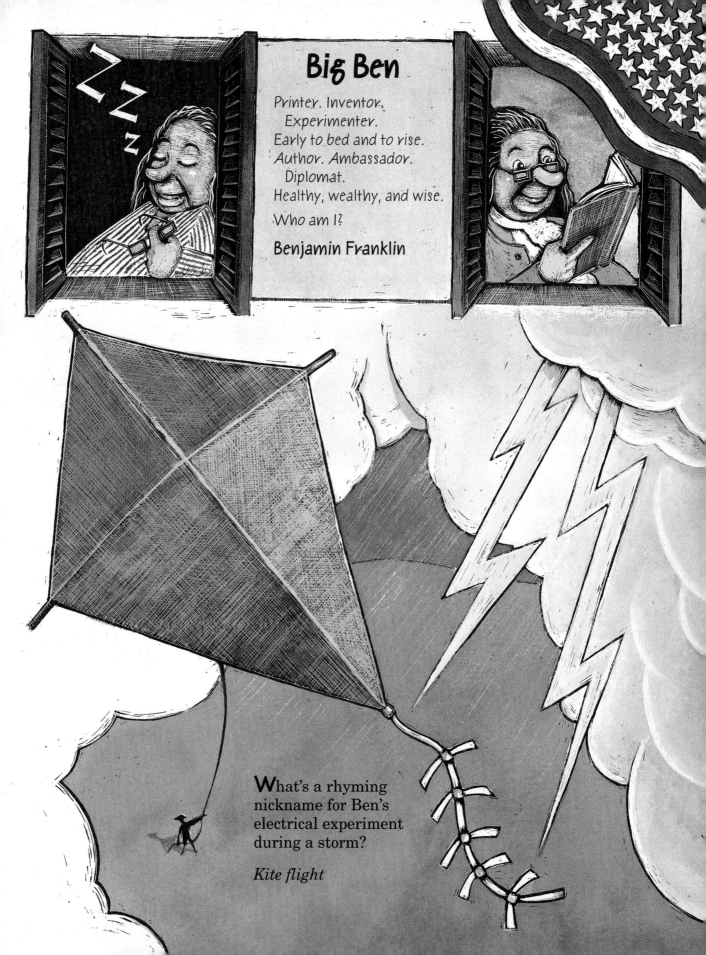

Big Ben

Printer. Inventor.
 Experimenter.
Early to bed and to rise.
Author. Ambassador.
 Diplomat.
Healthy, wealthy, and wise.

Who am I?

Benjamin Franklin

What's a rhyming nickname for Ben's electrical experiment during a storm?

Kite flight

Valley Forge George

The Revolutionary War—
    I helped to fight.
The Constitution—
    I helped to write.
Our country—
    I agreed to lead.
First president—
    admired indeed.

Who am I?

George Washington

Why was Washington's furniture so noisy?

Because his Cabinet was full of Secretaries (Secretary of State, Secretary of War, etc.).

Groovy Government

How is our government like a tree?

It has 3 branches: Executive, Judicial, Legislative.

What's a rhyming nickname for the White House?

President's residence

What does the American flag say when a president walks by?

Nothing. It just waves.

Talented Tom

He wrote the Declaration.
He lived at Monticello.
He served as *our* third president.
Who was this famous fellow?

Thomas Jefferson

Where did the Declaration of Independence get signed? *On the bottom*

Where was the Declaration of Independence written?

On a piece of paper

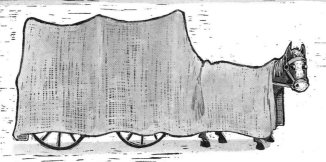

Covered Wagon

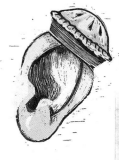

Pioneers (pie on ears)

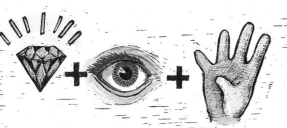

July 4th
(jewel eye 4th)

Buffalo Bill

Log Cabin

$+$ in

Rocky Mountains

$+$ E $+$

PICTURE

Columbus

Stagecoach

Dust Bowl

Underground
Railroad

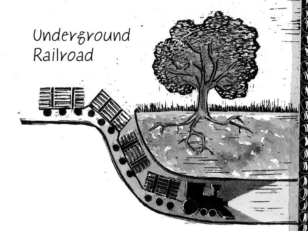

Wagon Train

Bald Eagle

RIDDLES

Sights to See

Who's That Lady?

There are people in my head.
They're staring from my crown.
There are stairs inside of me
for going up and coming down.
My right arm is getting pooped
from holding up this torch.
But I don't tire of visitors
arriving on my porch.

Who am I?

Statue of Liberty

A Welcoming Place

Welcome, ladies.
Welcome, gents.
Welcome, weary immigrants.
Welcome! Enter.
You can stay.
Welcome to the U.S.A.!

What am I?

Ellis Island

Seven continents.
Seven seas.
On my crown,
are seven of these:

Spikes

What's written
in bold on the
tablet I hold?

*July 4, 1776 (in
Roman numerals)*

Rocks in Their Heads
(To the tune of "Three Blind Mice")

Four Giant Heads.
Four Giant Heads.
See how we stare.
See how we stare.
We don't have shoulders or elbows or knees.
Our noses are almost as tall as the trees.
Better run for your life if we ever should sneeze.
Four Giant Heads.
Four Giant Heads.

What are we?

Mount Rushmore

We presidents
just watch and wait
high in the Black Hills
of what state?

South Dakota

Chief Relief

These presidents are not alone.
Sculptors are working stone by stone
to carve a nearby rock relief
of this Native American chief.

Who is it?

Crazy Horse

How are the Liberty Bell
and a duck alike?

They both have a quack.

What's round,
a symbol of the president,
and goes "Arp! Arp!"?

The Presidential Seal

Heading West

Teamwork

In 1804,
we went west to explore—
from the Missouri River
to the Oregon shore.

Who are we?

Lewis and Clark

Follow the Native American Leader

Follow me, Lewis.
Follow me, Clark.
I'll show you the way
through the forest so dark.
I'll lead you along
rapid rivers of blue.
And I'll guide you well
till your travels are through.

Who am I?

Sacajawea

Why did the MISSOURI River
have to
get glasses?

*Because it had
2 eyes but still
couldn't see.*

Wagons Ho!

Westward Ho!
We all go.
Wagons slow.
Oxen tow.
Campfires glow.
Harsh winds blow.
Rations low.
Frightened so—
turn back? No!
Forward. Yo!
New land. Oh!
Wagons, whoa!

Who are we?

Pioneers

What are 6 things most pioneers took traveling from Missouri to Oregon on the Oregon Trail?

Months

Name That American Invention

Thinner Dinner

"Slice my taters even thinner!" said the diner during dinner.

"Thin potatoes? How absurd! You won't like them, mark my word."

Crunch!

"I love them! They're great thinner! This invention is a winner!"

Potato chips
Invented by George Crum in Saratoga Springs, New York (1853)

We All Scream for Waffles?

Out of dishes? Oh, how awful! Scoop the ice cream in a waffle.

Ice cream cone
Invented at the World's Fair in St. Louis, Missouri (1904)

Oh, Nuts!

Nuts for me. Nuts for you. I'll show the world what nuts can do.

Over 300 peanut products
Developed by George Washington Carver (early 1900s)

Plane Talk

The Wright brothers built the first successful engine-powered airplane. Right or wrong?

Right.

Yes, Wright. Now answer me. Right or wrong?

First successful airplane flight
Completed by Orville and Wilbur Wright at Kitty Hawk, North Carolina (1903)

Know-how

Who had the know-how to know how to sew? Howe!

Lockstitch sewing machine
Invented by Elias Howe (1846)

How did Elias Howe like inventing?

Sew-sew.

Throw Out the Candles

My idea is
very bright.
It will set the
world alight.

Reliable electric light
Developed by
Thomas A. Edison (1879)

Hello?

Dial it. Punch it.
Give me a ring.
Call my number
on this thing.

Telephone
Invented by
Alexander Graham Bell
(1876)

No Seeds Needed

The seeds must be removed
after cotton is picked.
My invention proved
I've got this problem licked.

Cotton gin
Invented by Eli Whitney (1793)

Steam Dream

I dream that steam
will float a boat.

**First long-distance
steamboat**
Invented by Robert Fulton
(1807)

Play Ball!

Grab peach baskets.
Toss in a ball.
My new sport
is fun for all.

Basketball
Invented by
P.E. teacher
James Naismith (1891)

Message

Dot dash dash
dash dash dot—
what a good
idea I've got.

Morse code telegraph
Invented by Samuel Morse (1837)

Gold Fever

What's the Rush?

You'll never guess
what I've been told:
In them thar streams,
there's lots of gold.
At Sutter's Mill—
or so they say—
James Marshall struck
it rich one day.
I'm heading west,
quick as I can,
with my best mule
and my tin pan.
Some folks call me
forty-niner,
but I'm just a...

Gold Rush Miner

What's a miner's favorite game?

Hide and gold seek

What do you
call a miner
who complains?

A whiner miner

It's something a miner
needs to find gold.
If you add a C,
a chicken does it.
If you add a P,
it's done to a chicken.

Luck
(C + luck = Cluck
(P + luck = Pluck)

Boooom Towns?

Boom towns. Mining towns.
Dry goods. Chow.
Blacksmiths. Laundries.
What's there now?

Ghost Towns

A Nugget of Wisdom:

You can pick your friends.
You can pick your claim.
But you can't pick your
friend's claim. Or else!

What do miners look for in the winter?

Cold gold

What do you get if you cross a flag with a miner?

A star-spangled panner

Let's Get Connected

Giddy-up

Got mail.
Can't fail to deliver.
Can't stop.
Must ford through this river.
Can't slow
for snow, though I shiver.
Can't heed
my steed's legs that quiver.
Got mail.
Can't fail to deliver.

What am I?

A Pony Express Rider

How much did it cost to mail a letter by Pony Express?

A few horse cents

What was Pony Express mail carried in?

A nag bag

U.S. MAIL

What did Pony Express riders ride after dark?

Nightmares

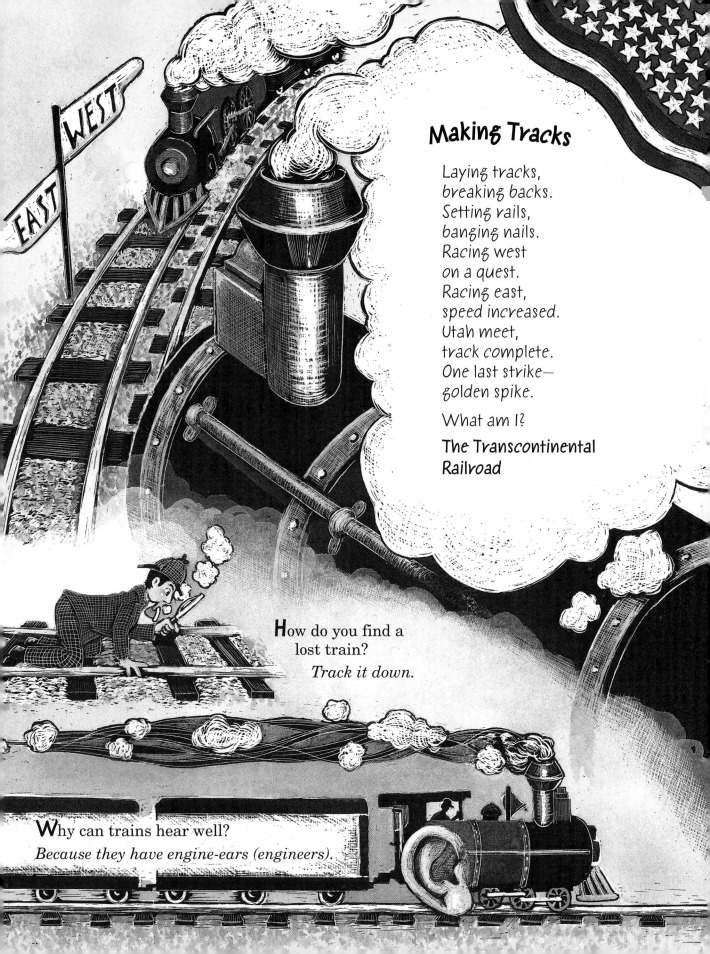

Making Tracks

Laying tracks,
breaking backs.
Setting rails,
banging nails.
Racing west
on a quest.
Racing east,
speed increased.
Utah meet,
track complete.
One last strike—
golden spike.

What am I?

The Transcontinental Railroad

How do you find a
lost train?
Track it down.

Why can trains hear well?
Because they have engine-ears (engineers).

It's Not Easy Being President

Tug of War

North: No slaves.
South: Plantations!
Disagreement.
Split. Two nations.

North: Come back!
South: No way!
Union blue.
Rebels gray.

North: Go, Grant!
South: Go, Lee!
Brothers fight.
Slaves go free.

North: Unite!
South: You win.
States together.
Whole again.

What am I?

The Civil War

I was the sixteenth president.
Today my face is on a cent.

Who am I?

Abraham Lincoln

Guess Which Prez Says . . .

I love honey!
Rutherford Bee (B.) Hayes

$2 + 2 = 4$
John Ad-ams

I am not happy.
James Mad-ison

My dentist says I've got cavities.
Millard Fill-more

If I had a canoe, I'd paddle.
Wood-row Wilson

I'm never warm.
Calvin Cool-idge

I make my own suits.
Zachary Tailor (Taylor)

I can fit 8 people in my vehicle.
Martin Van Buren

I can do 2,000 pounds of laundry.
George Washing-ton

I never fib.
Harry Tru-man

Nothing's ever easy for me!
Warren G. Hard-ing

I like owls!
Herbert Hoo-ver

The Wild West

Please Excuse the Sheriff!

Wild West sheriff.
Best friend, Bat.
Rules Dodge City.
Bad guys, scat!
Grabs the outlaws.
Bop! Bop! Bop!
Eats some lunch.
Swigs soda pop.

Buuuurp!
Pardon me!

Wild West sheriff.
Who is he?

Wyatt Earp

What's a nickname for a sheriff who drinks too much soda pop? *Wyatt Burp*

Why did the sheriff go to a gas station?

Because his ten-gallon hat was on empty.

What wears a tall hat, a star, sits in a saddle, and groans?

A sheriff with homework

Knock, knock.
Who's there?
Rodeo hee.
Rodeo hee who?
I didn't know you could yodel.

Knock, knock.
Who's there?
Ya.
Ya who?
Yahoo! Let's rodeo!

What did the horse say when the cowboy told it to jump the Grand Canyon?

Neigh.

Ya-hoo Am I?

Yee-hah! Howdy!
Come enjoy my show.
Cowboys. Cowgirls.
A Wild West rodeo.

Ropin'. Ridin'.
Furry critters, too.
Horses. Lassoes.
Lots of fun. Yahoo!

Who am I?

Buffalo Bill Cody

Famous Firsts

Outstanding

First lunar landing,
Neil Armstrong commanding,
what was left standing...
on the moon?

The United States flag
The first landing on the Moon.
(1969)

A Woman with Wings

The first female pilot to go
across the Atlantic solo.
Years later, when I made a flight,
my plane and I dropped out of sight.

Who am I?

Amelia Earhart
The first female pilot to fly alone across
the Atlantic Ocean nonstop.
(1932)

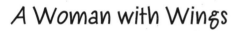

The Spirit of St. Louis

Across the Atlantic, I was first to fly.
From New York, I waved good-bye.
I could not sleep. I did not dare.
I must keep my plane in the air.
Nonstop to France my plane did go.
Crowds cheered for me, a great hero.

Who am I?

Charles Lindbergh
The first pilot to fly alone across
the Atlantic Ocean nonstop.
(1927)

Judge

Born in Texas. Raised on a ranch.
I serve in the judicial branch.
The first woman ever on the Supreme Court,
I judge law cases of the serious sort.

Who am I?

Sandra Day O'Connor
The first woman appointed to
the United States Supreme Court.
(Appointed in 1981)

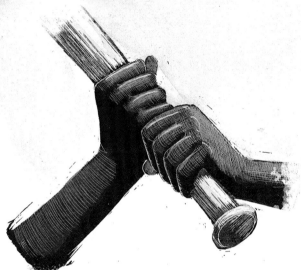

Rookie of the Year

First African-American ever to play
in major league baseball in my day.
I played the game that was my dream,
on the Brooklyn Dodgers team.

Who am I?

Jackie Robinson
The first African-American to play on
a major league baseball team.
(Started in his first major league
game in 1947.)

Native American Ballerina

Born and trained in the U.S.A.
<u>The Firebird</u>. <u>Swan Lake</u>. Grand jeté.

Who am I?

Maria Tallchief
Considered the first great prima ballerina
born and trained in the United States.
(Danced in the New York City Ballet's production
of <u>The Firebird</u>—the role for which she is best known—in 1949.)

Teacher, teacher, you did great!
I think your guesses were first rate.
You passed my riddle mystery.
Now this class is dismiss-tory . . .

and this old book is history!